n[illegible]

Darren C. Demaree

Harbor Editions
Small Harbor Publishing

neverwell

Cover art by Laura Page
Cover design by Allison Blevins
Book layout by Allison Blevins and Ellie Davis

NEVERWELL
DARREN C. DEMAREE
ISBN 978-1-957248-11-0
Harbor Editions,
an imprint of Small Harbor Publishing

This book is for my wife, Emily, my sister, Sarah, and my oldest daughter, Isabelle—the first three reasons why I'm sober.

Contents

neverwell

I have gone back
to the Giant Eagle
where once I drank
an open beer
in the cereal aisle
while my baby
daughter watched me
from her buckled seat.
I am gone there
forever in her eyes.
She doesn't remember
anything from that aisle
of our lives, but I can
still see her face hover
above the silver can
while I almost made
our store trip
a permanent record.

One by one I am
remembered
as a good man
by those who know
me sober. How
often I flail
for one more
act to counter
any decision
I made without
an audience.
If you have
questions about
my kindness,
know that you
should ask them.
I give these
answers with-
out prompting
most of the time.

Let me be clear:
I got off easy
& I do not trust
this reality that
took so little
from me. I was
a monster kept
in a basement
most of the time.
We moved out
of that house.
I will never leave
that house.
I buried myself
amidst white
cinderblock.
I promised nobody
that I would do
such a thing.
Regardless
& regardless
& regardless.

I always stay
on the porch
of the party.
I don't know
your house.
I am absolutely
hiding from
the conceit that
I'm to let loose.
I stay with
the children
at the party.
They do not
offer me beer
without ask-
ing about
the horrors
of being offered
a beer, about
being considered
rude or weird
or aloof or just
an asshole.
I don't trust
your house.
It's simple.
Spare me.
Spare me,
please. I can-
not spare myself.

I choke pillows
at night. I fight
back all the time.
I am not young
enough to survive
being taken
again. It's late
evening here
& I know how
un-safe that is.

A car skids
onto our
front lawn
& I rush out
to make sure
I'm not in it.

I cannot
tell you
what today
is. I can
only tell
you what
it is not.
Follow me
through
the small
& exact
syllables.
I pronounce
each one.
Not today.
Not today.

Why obscure
the fountain?
Any water
can be play-
ed in. Any water
can well
up. Why not
be public
with the true
romance
of your addict-
ion? Lungs
don't work
that way. Gasp-
ing is a show.
I am dry all
the time
because my only
other option
is to be wet
all the time.
I can't quite
explain my own
breathing.
I can tell you
my bathing suits
are a cry
for real help.

There are only
so many words
I have left
before I drink
again. I do not
propose to waste
any of them
on a prayer.
I refuse to waste
my clean love
on selfish,
impossible asks.

The witness suffers
differently. Witness
me suffer in my own,
comfortable ways.
These traditions
are short enough
for any tombstone.
The witness suffers
the surprise of my
survival. That good
is heavy enough
to bury us all in
a potential future.

I cling to my own
body. If I were to
hold another body
who would hold
on to mine? That
is the direct hit
of my marriage.
I am on the tip
of her tongue
all of her time.
It has to be ex-
hausting to be ex-
clusively present.

I appreciate the black
that can drag across
the whole of the past,
that can erase, that
can show the erasing,
but if I were to call
any of that thick dark
something other than
a consequence, would
you believe me? I can
write about the sun
at night, but what
happened during
the day matters more
if any part of our life
is about survival.

I have shown
that I will
drink anything.
No one can
teach me how
to prove
the opposite.
I am thirsty
all the time. I
don't know what
that proves.

It was not
unforgiveable
to take the beer
my toddler
brought me
from the room-
temperature
cardboard box
I kept in her toy
bin. That happened.
She knew
what I wanted
& she was strong
enough to bring
the can all the way
to my unsteady
nature. The wreck-
age, the infinite re-
play of wreckage
that still wakes
me is exactly how
strong she got
through the un-
ending process.

I love songs
that never end
& never pardon.

The cold water
shocks before it
caves the walls
of your heart.
I remember
alcohol never
left me quite so
shivering. The piss,
on the other hand,
in the morning—
on the high count
sheets my wife
bought for our bed—
that was a god-
damn earthquake.

Shatter to shatter,
I walk on glass
all the time. Glass
is slowly becoming
the sand of a beach
I'll be buried under—
the only promise
I've given
to my own body.
That promise
is what I have left.

I have almost eight years
of sober thoughts
& all of them
curve my hips back
to the past where I was
a body in a basement
that refused to rise
because of a trauma
I could not think
to frame my mouth
around. That partial
guilt gives me what now?
All the names
tattooed on my body
have propped me up
for years, so maybe no one
put me in that basement.
Maybe it was the safest
place to be a drunk?
I am the whole village fed
for weeks by this
temporary belief
& I confess, actual hunger
has to started to braid me.

My ego had me
believe
the landscape
was a landscape
only. What
terrible narrative
a single human
remains to be.

You cannot tell
your children
the home you made
for them to grow up
in can never be
your home
because you have
an unassailable talent
for fidgeting in
your skin, for fight-
ing default. You prefer
to burn down everything
given to you.
You cannot tell
your children
you are never whole
enough to give them
two open hands
because one fist must
be clamped on your
throat at all times.
They won't
read this poem,
but if they do, it won't
make any sense.
Love
is quite real.

Cold water eases
over the heavy parts
of my past. A river?
Drag the river.
Am I still in it?
Hold my drowning
as a baptism.
All I promised
was that I would
dump the whiskey.

There are four stores
I do not enter anymore.
If I did the owners
would put a twelve-
pack of Pabst
& a sixer of Burning
River on the counter
next to a bottle
of champagne
& they would
expect to see me
again the next day.
There are four stores
I do not enter anymore.

I've been waiting
for a collection
of poetry about
addiction that holds
no metaphors at all.
I do not believe
I am owed the coat
of language.
I've learned to flare
at my best when
I talk about how
close I came
to killing more
than myself
during some
of those drives
I took when I was
challenged to prove
I was truly sober.

Not a single word
on my suicide attempts
has made it into
the memoir I'm writing.
I chose the beginning
& the ending, so
my children would
not have to carry
my temporary nature
with them forever.

I was rendered
under a giant
orange construction
sign. The black
paths of my tires
were still smoking
as I looked up
at the closed road
sign between
Wooster
& Mount Vernon
& if the sign had
taken the windshield
out (inches as it was
from doing so)
it would have taken
my head with it.
I remember
the burnt smell
& that the old police
car I was driving
had no airbags.
I remember that
I turned around
without incident
& made it back
to the Wooster
Taco Bell
without getting
arrested or dead.
So many signs
try to sell you
a version of truth.
I was never
a close reader.

My births
have all
been steady.
It's the dying
I can't do
for shit.
It's the living
I can't apple.

I rose without
feeling. I rose
without choice.
It was better that
way. All of my
choices were made
by the ounce.

I know how best
not to dream
at night. I know
the dust, no matter
how much sweep-
ing I do, remains
in the air.
I live, necessarily,
without a picture
of the hole
behind my eyes.
I speak quietly
all the time.
I'm not supposed
to be thought of
in the morning.

Most of my wanting
is lost in the translation
from Ohio to Ohia.

Turn on
the lights.
I don't scurry
anymore.

I know most history
is lattice-work. God-
damn if mine isn't
just a knotted
rope that dangles.

I breathe
well. I want
too much
to remain
with the air.
The lunge eats
the lungs
every time.

Painting
the rocks
does nothing
if that is
the path
you fall onto
every time,
but look,
look, look
how pretty
my body is
amidst
the letting,
& the letting go.

I have lived
two lives
in one world.
Look at me.
My face
is all petals
but no bloom.

I sleep at night.
You have
no idea the sort
of deals I've made
to be able
to sleep at night.
I earned this
sobriety by sell-
ing everything
I owned with-
out asking
for money back.

I know that flash
of teeth that makes
most men look
like they want
to eat the world.
I have seen it as most
men have looked
at me the same way.
If we meet, if I see
your eyes, know
that I've looked
at your eyes, that
I have ignored your
mouth entirely.
There is only one
mouth can consume
me. It has no throat.
It spits me back
every time. I fear
only my own
invitation. The rest
of the men
in this world have
taken their shot.

I have been found
too often by mornings
that wish
me lost forever. I
cannot hide. I can
make sure you know
where to look for me.
I am sitting here
in anticipation
of my own weakness.
Please send everyone.

You can breathe
through a bottle
if you break it.

Cold water torments
the field beneath
the bloom. I love
that metaphor. I get
to see the silvering
beauty. I am
with the flood.
I have always been
with the flood.
The folks in town
know this about me.
They, lovingly, lay
sandbags at my feet.

I am dry.
Was I in-
tended
to become
my own
deep dust?

I was never lured
into the slaughter
of my own body.
That shit was my idea.
I have survived
despite my
executioner hiding
behind my own hood.

Lips think
only of lips.
I am a drunk.
I think only
of what
I am drinking.
Right now,
it is water,
but I don't trust
this fucking
cup. It could
hold anything.

I have a whole life
outside
this wreckage,
but I don't like
how few names
it has for me.
Call me all
of what I am.
It's safer that way.

My nights
are their own
books. This,
this, this is
the whole book
of my days.

I trust my tongue.
It never let me swallow
it completely. I tried.

I am laced
at this point
& yet I am
taken in daily
by those
that love me.
It doesn't feel
right to me.
I am loved
& does that
mean love
is inherent?
I haven't earned
a single thing.

I am held
in this moment.
No. That
would be
lovely. I hold
this moment.

Don’t you think
if I had
an agent, I could
simplify this world,
have them
release one state-
ment about me,
my love of not
transcending
& then you all
could help me
stay here, sober
& safe forever?

I wish I was alive
in a different way.

If I told you
the landscape
of Ohio
was beautiful
while my mouth
was full of petals,
would you offer
me a drink?
I could eat
Ohio for a drink
right now.
I am afraid
of swallowing
Ohio.
If I am ever
too quiet
for too long,
send Kentucky.

I care for music.
No. I am afraid
of thick silence.

We named
the seasons
too plainly.

The list of things
I don't need to know
is much longer
than the list of things
I have swallowed
so that I can know
them exactly.
I am skinnier now.
That does not mean
I am happier.

A spun wheel
buries us all
for a little bit.

The dark tunnels
as much as the light
tunnels. I do not
fear what floods
out of me anymore.
I hold myself
still regardless
of what you see
collecting on the edge
of our property.

I have never been
invited into the sublime.
I have framed
facsimiles for those
I love most—
my gift shows
how almost beautiful
the world can be
when I can find
the proper wood
to seal it in.
I do not hang anything.
I collect the nails
to keep the nails away.
I promise nothing.
I am loved for acting
outside of promises.

Honey blackens
if you allow the charcoal
to dissolve in the bottle.
Nitroglycerin
did nothing to change
my chemistry. I am alive.
Sweetness
has hidden, elsewhere.

Like a snow
that lasted too long.
Like we got
desperate, so we tried
to keep some
in our bellies. I floated
here. I know
I will drink
again some day.
Some parts of this
world aren't a season.

# Acknowledgements

Grateful acknowledgment is made to the editors of the following journals, who published these poems, or earlier versions of them:

North Dakota Quarterly
Great Lakes Review
The Mantle Poetry
Cortland Review
Rabble Review

Darren C. Demaree is the author of nineteen poetry collections, most recently *neverwell* (Harbor Editions, 2023). He is the recipient of a Greater Columbus Arts Council Grant, an Ohio Arts Council Individual Excellence Award, the Louise Bogan Award from Trio House Press, and the Nancy Dew Taylor Award from *Emrys Journal.* He is the Editor-in-Chief of the *Best of the Net Anthology* and the Managing Editor of *Ovenbird Poetry*. He is currently living in Columbus, Ohio with his wife and children.

Made in the USA
Monee, IL
09 March 2025